BARACK OBAMA

AMERICA'S FIRST AFRICAN-AMERICAN PRESIDENT

Biography Of Presidents

Children's Biography Books

BABY PROFESSOR
EDUCATION KIDS

Speedy Publishing LLC
40 E. Main St. #1156
Newark, DE 19711
www.speedypublishing.com
Copyright 2017

In this book, we're going to talk about the life of Barack Obama, who was the United States President for eight years. So, let's get right to it!

PRESIDENT BARACK OBAMA was the first African-American to gain the Presidential office. A highly intelligent, charismatic president, he was first elected to office in 2008, and also was elected in 2012 to serve a second term in office.

Barack Obama

Hawaii

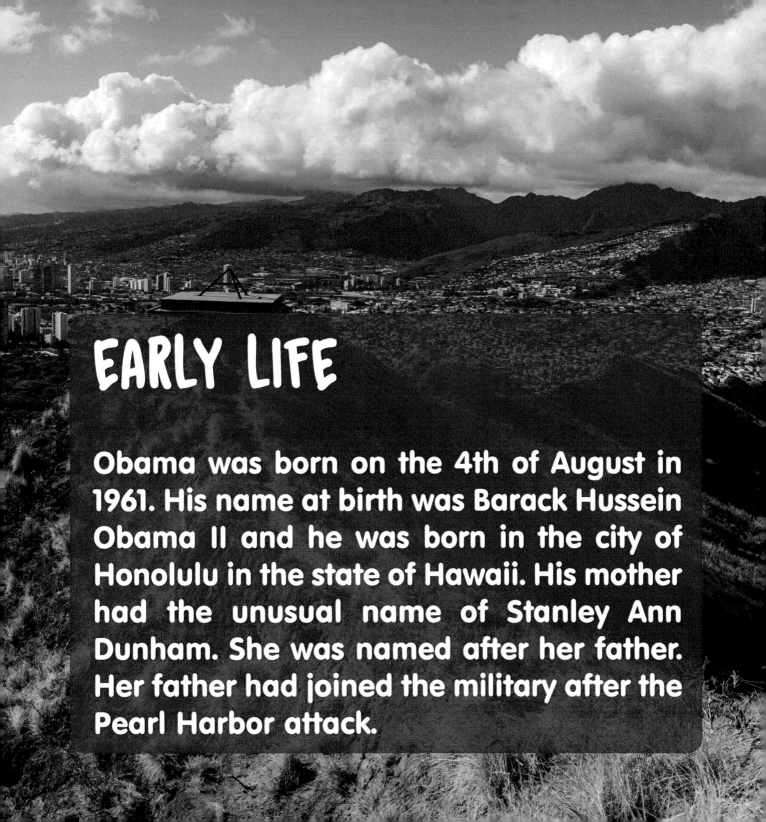

EARLY LIFE

Obama was born on the 4th of August in 1961. His name at birth was Barack Hussein Obama II and he was born in the city of Honolulu in the state of Hawaii. His mother had the unusual name of Stanley Ann Dunham. She was named after her father. Her father had joined the military after the Pearl Harbor attack.

He served under General George Patton during World War II. Stanley Ann's mother, Obama's grandmother, was named Madelyn, and during the war she worked on an assembly line where she helped to construct bombers. Madelyn gave birth to Stanley Ann when the couple was stationed at the Wichita Army base in Kansas. When the war was over, Stanley Ann's parents bought a house and after they moved several times, they ended up in Hawaii.

General George Patton

University of Hawaii

When Stanley Ann was college age she became a student at the University of Hawaii in Manoa. There, she met Barack Obama Senior. Obama Sr. was born in Kenya and had grown up taking care of herds of goats. He had big dreams and wanted to go to Hawaii to study. He worked hard and earned a scholarship.

Stanley Ann, who was Caucasian, and Barack Obama Senior, who was a black African from the Luo tribe, met and fell in love at the university. They married in 1961 and Barack Junior was born that same year. However, Barack's parents didn't stay together very long.

3RD WIFE'S
HUT

Luo Village

View of Jakarta City, Indonesia

Barack was raised by his mother. When Barack was still a toddler, his father went to Massachusetts to attend Harvard. His parents divorced in March of 1964. Soon after the divorce was finalized Obama Senior went back to Kenya. A year later, Barack's mother married an Indonesian student, Lolo Soetoro and the family moved to Jakarta, the capital city of Indonesia. Barack's half-sister, Maya Soetoro Ng was born there five years later, in 1970. His mother was worried about Barack's safety in Indonesia so she sent him back to Hawaii to live with her parents. Later, Barack's mother and half-sister joined him back in the United States.

Punahou Academy in Honolulu

BARACK'S EDUCATION

While living in Hawaii with his grandfather and grandmother, Obama, who was nicknamed Barry, became a student at the Punahou Academy. He was an excellent student as well as a great basketball player and he graduated with honors in 1979. There were only three African-American students at the Academy and Obama struggled with his identity as a child of two different races.

Car damaged by accident on the road

He often wondered if he would ever fit in. His father's absence didn't help his sense of self. Obama Sr. had only come back to Hawaii for one short visit in 1971. Obama couldn't understand why his father wouldn't stay in Hawaii.

Obama was only 21 years old when his father died in a car crash in 1982. It was the second time he had been in a crash. He had lost both of his legs in a serious accident just the year before.

After Obama graduated from high school, he went to Los Angeles. He studied at Occidental College for two years and then left for New York City to study at Columbia University.

Residential street in the city of Chicago

He graduated with a political science degree and went to work in business for two years before moving to Chicago. When he arrived there in 1985, at the age of 24, he began to work as a community coordinator for residents with low-incomes. He worked in the communities of Roseland as well as Altgeld Gardens.

LAW CAREER

Even though Obama was not raised in a household where religion was practiced, he joined the Trinity United Church of Christ while he was living in Chicago. He also traveled to his father's side of the family in Kenya and visited his father's grave. It was a very emotional experience for him and he came back transformed and ready to start a new phase of his life.

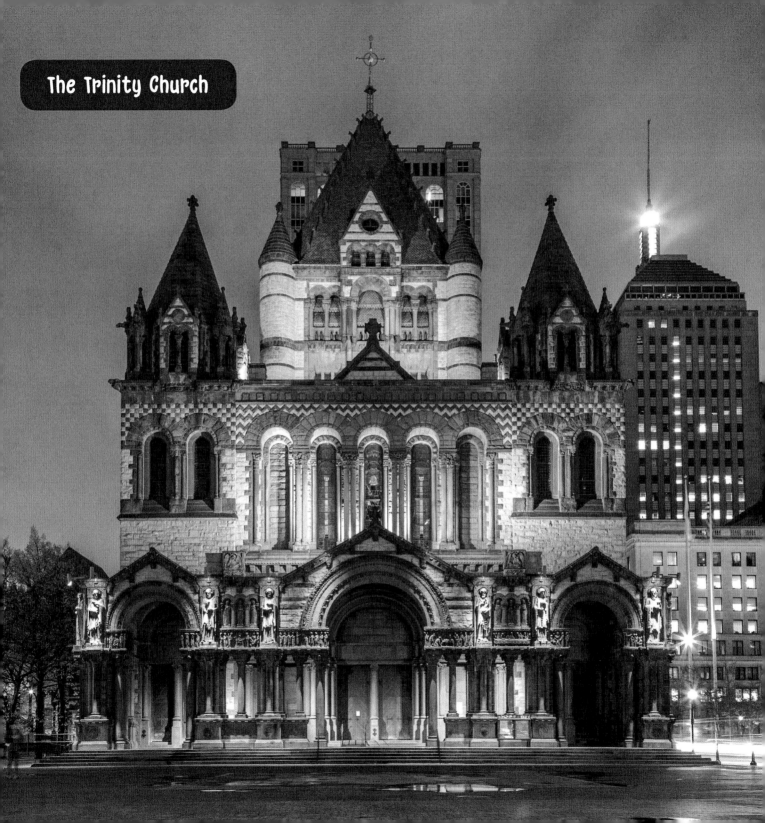

The Trinity Church

Harvard University campus

He was 27 years old when he entered Harvard Law School. The following summer he worked as an associate at Sidley Austin, a law firm in Chicago.

Another young lawyer, Michelle Robinson, was given the role as his adviser. Outside the office, Barack and Michelle began dating.

Michelle Robinson

They would eventually marry several years later and have two daughters. In 1990, he was elected a prestigious position as editor for the Harvard Law Review. He was the first African-American to have that role. He graduated and began practicing law at the age of 30.

SENATE CAREER

In 1996, at the age of 35, Barack chose to run for office. He made a run for the State Senate seat in the state of Illinois and was victorious. He served in Illinois as a senator for eight years and was then elected to serve as a senator in the US Senate.

Obama as Senator

He had held the office of United States Senator for three years when he campaigned for the 2008 election for United States President. Because of his intelligence, charisma, and cultured presence, he quickly gained admiration across the country. His polished speaking style and magnetic personality made him popular.

He went up against Hillary Clinton and won in the primaries. She had been a senator in the state of New York as well as the first lady when Bill Clinton was president. This win made him the Democratic candidate for president.

Hillary Clinton

In the final presidential election he was up against Republican John McCain. Obama won the run for President and took office in January of 2009. He was re-elected for a second term in 2012 when he ran against Mitt Romney who had been the Republican candidate.

BARACK OBAMA'S PRESIDENCY

Major events of Barack Obama's two terms in office are described below.

Wars in the country of Iraq and the country of Afghanistan had begun before Obama took office. The war in Iraq was somewhat successful and the United States troops were eventually brought home. However, the war in Afghanistan had increasing casualties through 2010.

Soldiers Marching

World Trade Center a few months before 9/11, New York.

The President worked with strategic teams to seek out Osama bin Laden, who was the mastermind of the attacks on the Twin Towers on 9/11. He was captured by special forces and killed in May of 2011.

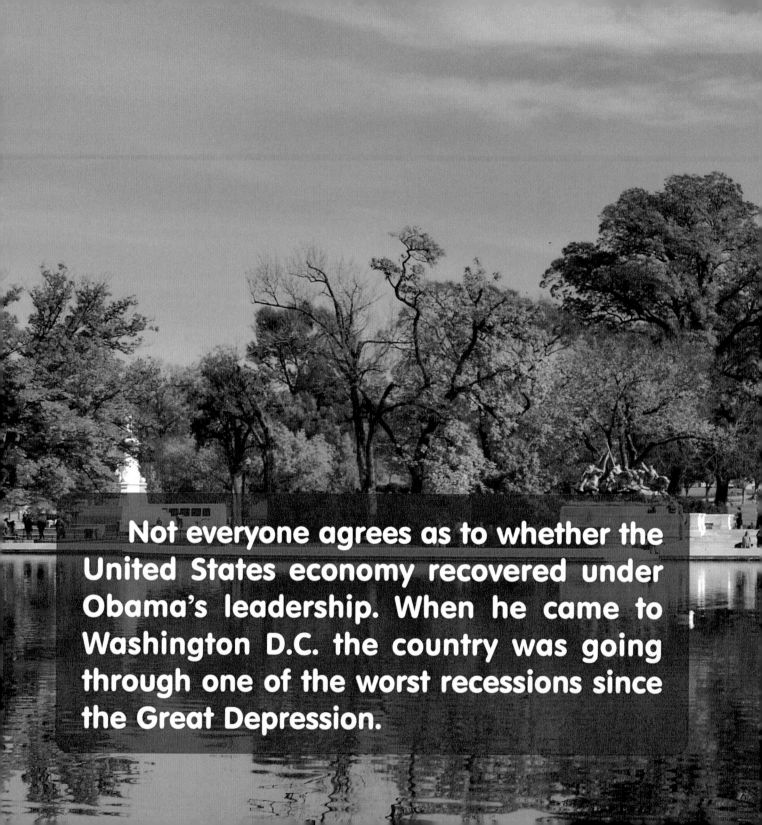

Not everyone agrees as to whether the United States economy recovered under Obama's leadership. When he came to Washington D.C. the country was going through one of the worst recessions since the Great Depression.

US Capitol Building in Washington D.C.

He proposed an increase in taxes as well as a more active role from the federal government. He put stimulus plans into place to jump start the economy into recovery. Despite these efforts, the economy only showed some signs of improvement. The nation's debt doubled during his two terms in office.

The President pushed for reforms in health care. The new law went into effect in 2010 and was frequently called "Obamacare" for short. The law was designed so that all Americans would have health care coverage but reactions to the plan have been mixed. Some citizens who had never had health care insurance before were finally able to pay for it and have coverage. Others who had coverage were not able to pay the now tripled premium rates and were forced to give it up and pay a penalty for not having it to the government. The idea of coverage for all was a good one, but it was not good for everyone.

Gulf Oil Spill

One of the worst environmental disasters in history happened during Obama's presidency. An accident in 2010 caused an enormous spill of oil in the Gulf of Mexico. The animals, plants, and people in the area are still suffering from the aftereffects.

President Obama was very successful in his work with other countries. He signed a nuclear agreement with the country of Iran. He ousted Moammar Gaddafi, the tyrannical Libyan leader. He also opened the door to more favorable policies with communist Cuba. Obama was the first president to visit the country of Cuba since the 1920s.

Habana, Cuba

AFTER HIS PRESIDENCY

President Obama and his family are traveling and enjoying their life together since he left office. He is writing books and speaking on a regular basis. As with other former presidents, he will more than likely play a part in global politics in the future.

FASCINATING FACTS ABOUT BARACK OBAMA

- He has made millions as an author and also won a Grammy for his voice on the book he wrote called Dreams From My Father.
- He can speak a little Spanish and is quite fluent in Indonesian.
- Because he worked in an ice-cream store for a long time as a teenager, he doesn't like ice cream anymore.

- He has read and reread all the Harry Potter novels.
- When he lived in Indonesia, he ate dog meat, snake meat, and crunchy grasshoppers.
- He still loves to play basketball. He also loves to cheer for the Chicago teams—the Chicago Bears and the Chicago White Sox, for football and baseball respectively.

Awesome! Now you know more about the life and career of President Barack Obama. You can find more Biography books from Baby Professor by searching the website of your favorite book retailer.

Made in the USA
Las Vegas, NV
30 April 2024

89326227R00040